DISCOVERING SHAPES

CIRCLES

SANDY RIGGS

ART BY RICHARD MACCABE

BENCHMARK BOOKS

MARSHALL CAVENDISH

NEW YORK

Benchmark Books
Marshall Cavendish Corporation
99 White Plains Road
Tarrytown, New York 10591-9001

©Marshall Cavendish Corporation, 1997

Series created by Blackbirch Graphics, Inc.

Printed and bound in the United States.

Library of Congress Cataloging-in-Publication Data

Riggs, Sandy
    Circles / by Sandy Riggs : art by Richard Maccabe.
        p.   cm. — (Discovering shapes)
    Includes index.
    Summary: Identifies different kinds of circles and discusses how they can be drawn and measured.
        ISBN 0-7614-0458-9 (lib. bdg.)
        1. Circle—Juvenile literature. [1. Circle.] I. Maccabe, Richard, ill. II. Title. III. Series.
    QA484.R54   1997
    793.7'4—dc20

                                                                96-1389
                                                                CIP
                                                                AC

Contents

Do You Know a Circle When You See One?

Look at this illustration of two circles. Is one circle larger than the other? Or are they both the same size?

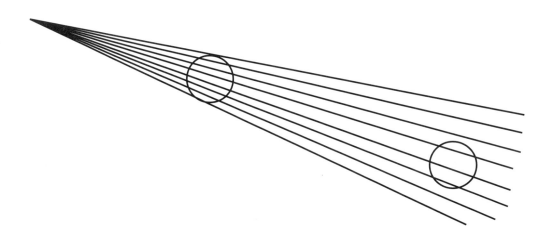

Now try this one. Are both of the inside circles the same size? Or is one smaller than the other?

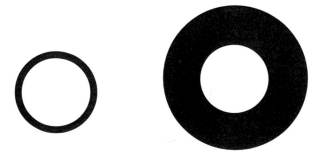

Are Circles Important?

Inventors of machines and designers of objects think circles are important. What do you think?

Make a list of circular objects. Can you make an A to Z list? Try it with a friend.

You can include circular objects, such as a yo-yo, or objects that have circular parts, such as an automobile.

I bet you a nickel there are some hints here.

Did you find making that list easy? Well, here's a challenge. Go on a circle hunt. Can you find 50 different circles? Make tally marks to record the circles you see.

Drawing Circles

Circles are not easy to draw. Try drawing some with one of the methods below. When you draw a circle you think is pretty good, cut it out.

You will need:

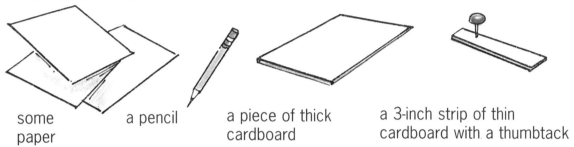

some   a pencil   a piece of thick   a 3-inch strip of thin
paper   cardboard   cardboard with a thumbtack

1. The Hand-Only Method
Pick up your pencil and draw a circle or two.

2. The Drawing-Around System
Find some circular things and draw around them.

3. The Cardboard-Strip Way
Put a sheet of paper on top of the thick cardboard. Poke a small hole in one end of the 3-inch strip of cardboard. Tack the other end of the strip to the paper. Put the pencil point in the hole and swing it around.

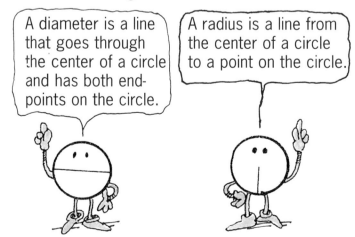

A diameter is a line that goes through the center of a circle and has both end-points on the circle.

A radius is a line from the center of a circle to a point on the circle.

• Now fold the circle you cut out to make a diameter and label the diameter.

• Find the center of the circle by folding and put a dot in the center. Are any of your fold lines a radius? Trace one and label it.

Think Fast

See how fast you can solve each puzzle. Use a clock or a watch with a second hand and write down your times. Then challenge friends to beat your times.

How many circles in all?

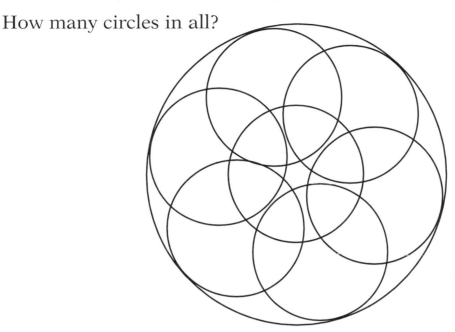

Which circles are linked?

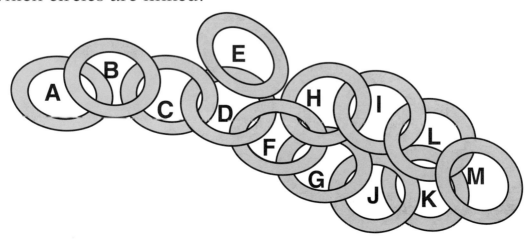

Compass Creations

One way to draw circles is to use a compass. Once you get the hang of it, you'll be drawing big circles, small circles, medium-sized circles, and circles on circles.

Get some scrap paper and practice using a compass. Then try copying this design. Follow the steps.

A compass is a tool for drawing circles. It holds a pencil.

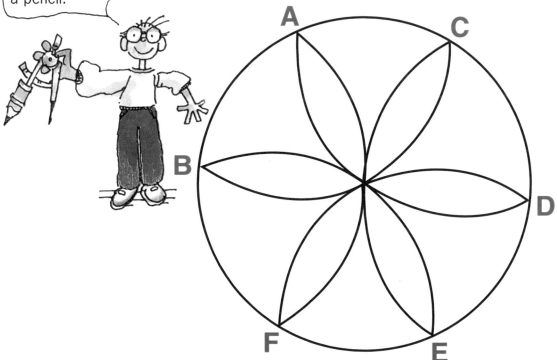

1. Draw a medium-sized circle.

2. Without changing the setting of the compass, place its point on the circle at point A.

3. Place the pencil at point B and draw a curved line inside the circle (BC).

4. Then place the compass point on C and the pencil on A. Draw another curved line (AD).

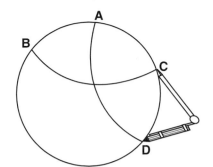

5. Move the compass point and draw more curves:

Move to D and draw CE.
Move to E and draw FD.
Move to F and draw BE.
Move to B and draw AF.

Now copy and color these compass creations.

marble

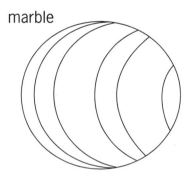

For some of the lines, change your compass setting a little.

beach ball

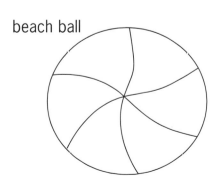

Mark the center of your circle. Draw from the center to the edge 6 times.

Wheels and Gears

One of the most important inventions in the history of the world is a circle: the wheel. Since its discovery about 5,000 years ago, the wheel has put people on the move—from the wooden wheels of ancient carts to the rubber tires of modern jets.

Add teeth to a wheel and it's a gear. Here's a gear wheel. Trace it on cardboard. Cut out two gears and fit the teeth together.

• What happens when you turn one gear?

• In what direction does each gear turn?

The moving parts of many machines are run by gears. Cars have gears. So do some clocks. And have you ever noticed the gear wheels on a bike?

Gears can change the speed of the moving parts. The size of the gear wheels makes a difference. What else might affect speed? Do you think the number of teeth in the gear wheels matters?

• Take one of your cardboard gears and cut off every other tooth so the gear has only six teeth. Fit the gears together and turn the gear with twelve teeth.

• Are the gear wheels turning at the same speed? How do the speeds compare?

Ready for a really hard question? Try to picture the gears below in motion. If gear A turns in a clockwise direction, in which direction does gear C turn?

Clockwise means moving in the direction that the hands of a clock move.

Can You Get In?

Which path will lead you to the center of the circle? See if you can see how to get there without touching the maze. Then move your finger around and around to check your answer.

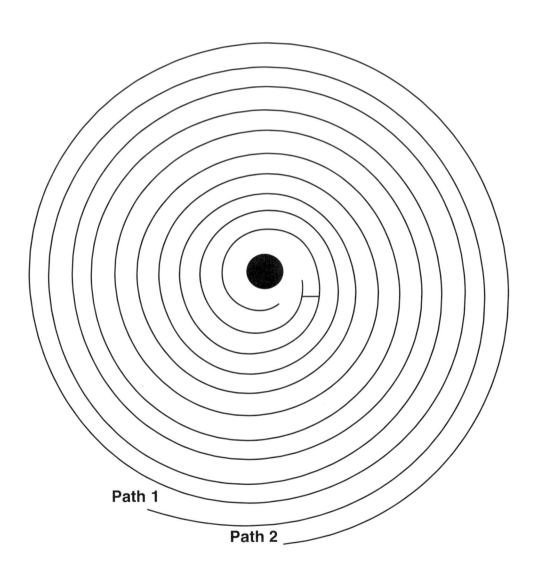

Path 1

Path 2

A Twisty Circle

Cut some scrap paper into two strips. Make each
strip about 2 inches wide and 14 inches long.
Draw a line down the middle of each strip.

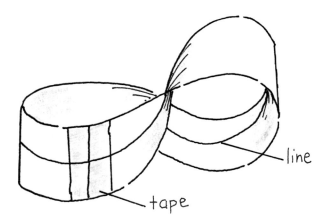

1. Take one of the strips. Twist it once and then
tape the ends together. This loop is called a
Moebius strip because a German mathematician
named August Ferdinand Moebius created it.

What do you think you will get if you cut this
strip along the center line? Now try it and see
if your prediction was right.

2. Take the other strip. Twist this strip two times
before taping the ends together. Then cut along
the line. What do you get? Amazing, isn't it?

Pedal Power

Play this game with a friend and take off on an imaginary cross-country bike race.

What you will need:

• a marker for each player (You could use buttons of different colors.)

• a number cube or one die from a pair of dice

A chord is a line with both endpoints on a circle.

How to play:

1. Put your markers on START.

2. Take turns throwing the die. If you throw a 1, 2, 3, or 4, move that number of spaces. If you throw a 5 or 6, take another turn.

3. When you land on a wheel space, answer the question or name the circle part. Use the circle in the top corner. If you're right, move ahead one more space.

4. If you land on a DOWNHILL space, an UPHILL space, or a FLAT TIRE space, do what it says.

5. Of course, the first racer to reach the FINISH LINE wins.

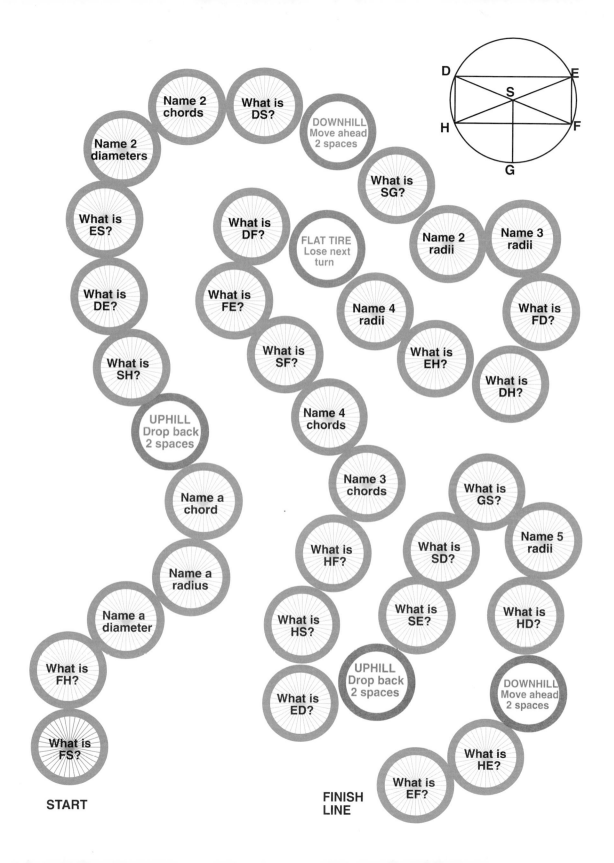

Tic-Tac-Toe in a Circle

Play a different kind of tic-tac-toe. Find a friend who is willing to go around in circles with you.

To begin:
• Trace each of the game boards on page 17 or draw your own. (Use a compass to draw the circles and a ruler to add the diameters.) If you want to play several games, draw several boards.
• Decide who will be **X** and who will be **O**.

To play:
• Take turns writing your mark in an empty space.
• Try to get three marks in a row, but remember to block the other player from doing so.

You can win by making a straight line *or* a curved line.

To win:
• If no player has three in a row after all spaces are filled, the game is a tie.
• The game ends when a player gets three in a straight line or three in a curved line. This player wins this game.

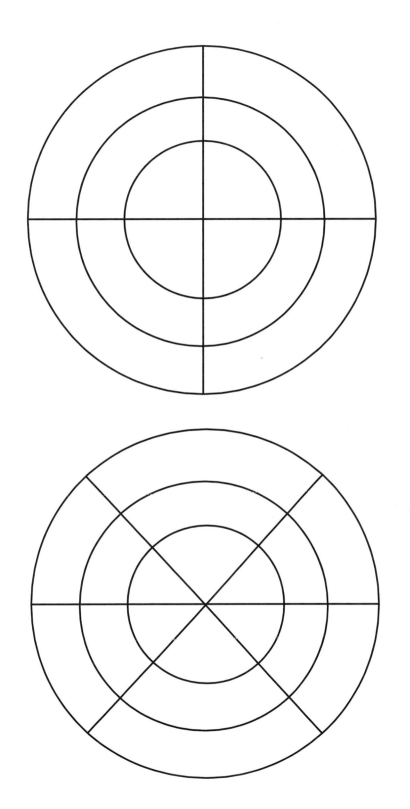

What's the Point?

A circle is a handy shape to use for drawing other shapes.
So try your hand at it.

Getting a Circle in Shape

1. First draw a circle with a radius of 13 cm. (The one shown is not to scale.)
2. Lightly draw two diameters to make fourths.
3. Then divide the circle into eighths. (Measure the distance between endpoints and find the middle.) Again, draw light lines.
4. You now have an 8-point circle. Label the points. Erase all the lines.

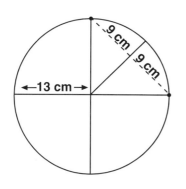

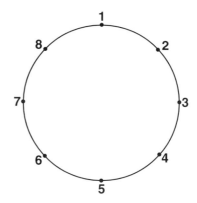

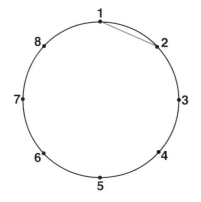

Using the Circle to Draw Shapes

Draw your lines with a ruler and use pencils of three colors. Use one color to connect all the points around the circle in order. The first one is done for you. What shape do you get? What color is it?

18

Now use a different color. Skip one point each time as you go around the circle. What's the shape?

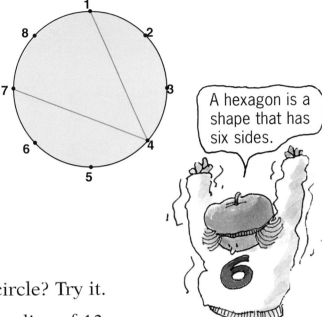

Using your last color, skip two points and draw. Do you see the star?

A hexagon is a shape that has six sides.

What if you used a 12-point circle? Try it.

• Draw another circle with a radius of 13 cm.

• Divide it into fourths.

• Then divide each fourth into three equal parts.

• Again, label the points and erase the lines.

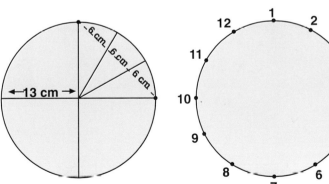

• What shape do you think you will draw if you skip three points? Do it. Did you guess the right shape?

• Can you draw a hexagon in the circle? Would you skip any points? If so, how many? Do it.

19

Eyeball Benders

Do you see the circles in these designs? The circles have been split into fourths and put into corners. One design in each row matches the circle. Can you find it?

1.

A　　　　　B　　　　　C

2.

A　　　　　B　　　　　C

3.

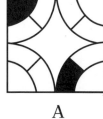   

A　　　　　B　　　　　C

Fix your eyeballs on these circles for a while.
Which design has more blue in it?

A

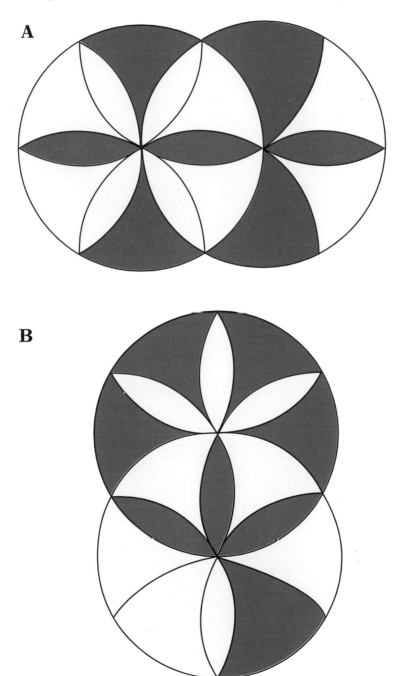

B

Congruent or Concentric?

This game of congruent and concentric circles is not hard to play. It's just hard to say. Are you game to play? Okay. Two can play.

You will need:

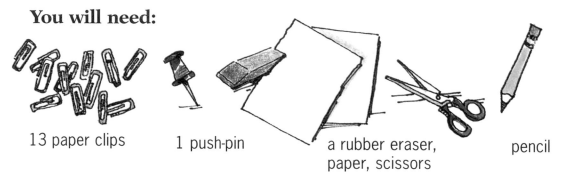

13 paper clips   1 push-pin   a rubber eraser, paper, scissors   pencil

Make a spinner. Draw and cut out a circle. Divide it into four parts and write the numbers 1, 2, 3, 4. Attach a paper clip to the center with the push-pin. Put the eraser under the paper and stick the point of the pin into it.

How to play:
- Cover each space on the game board with a clip.
- Take turns spinning the spinner.
- If you spin a **1**, take a clip from a set of concentric circles.
- If you spin a **2**, take clips from a pair of congruent circles.
- If you spin a **3**, lose this turn.
- If you spin a **4**, spin again.
- Play until all the clips have been taken.
- The player with the most clips is the winner.

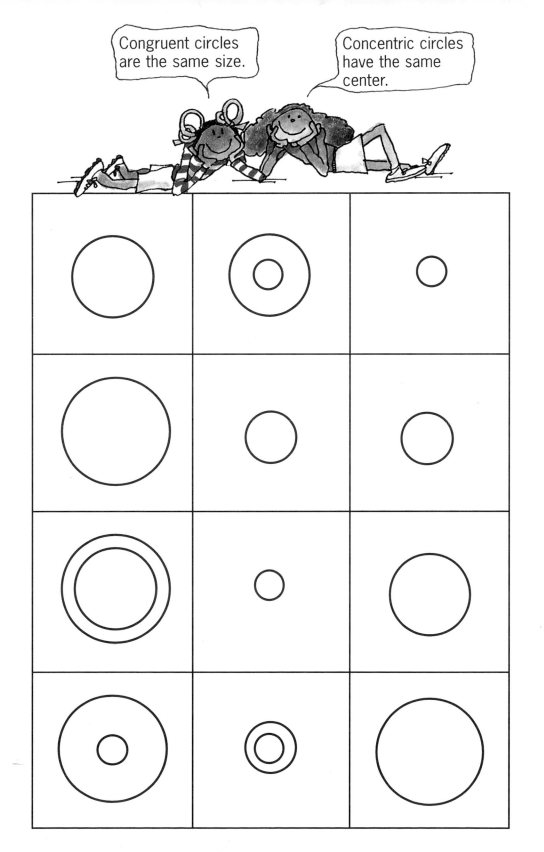

Pi = 3.14

Pizza "Pi"

Pizza pie is a circle of dough often covered with a spicy sauce, cheese, and pepperonis. Mathematical pi is a number. You can use it to figure out how big around circular things are—circular things like pizzas and pepperonis. Use pi to play this game with a friend.

Get Ready
You'll need a calculator, a penny, and fifteen game markers each (two different colors).

Get Set
To find the distance around a circle, do this:
• Multiply **pi x diameter,** or
• Multiply **2 x pi x radius.**
• When you play, use the calculator. Check your answers at the back of the book.

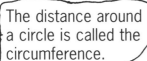

The distance around a circle is called the circumference.

Go!
• Take turns flipping or spinning the penny.
• If it lands heads up, figure out the circumference of one pepperoni. If you're correct, cover it with a marker.
• If it lands tails up, figure out the circumferences of two pepperonis. If you're correct, cover both.
• Play until all pepperonis are covered.
• The player who covers the most pepperonis wins.

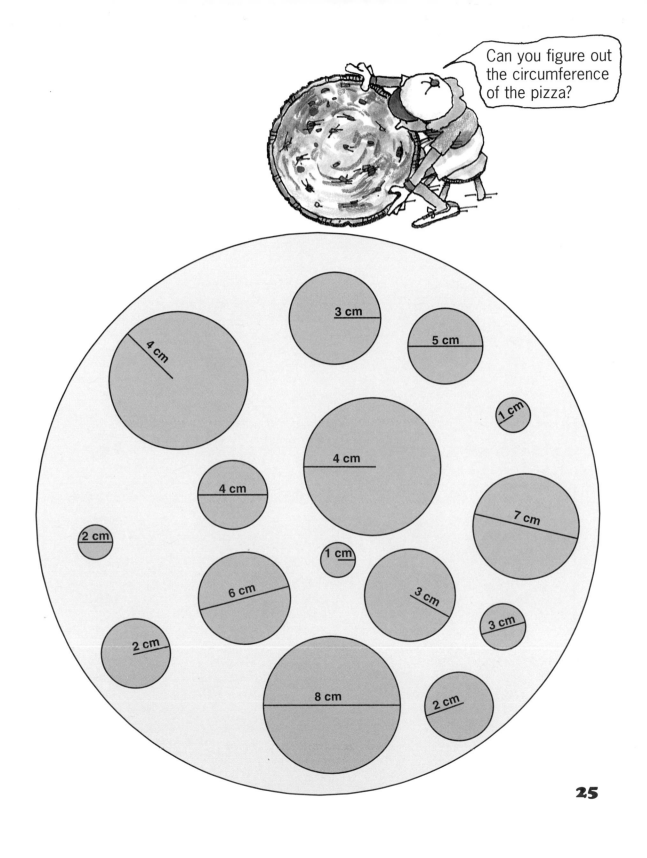

Dot and Dart Boards

Draw a dot board like the one here—only bigger.
Make five rows of dots. Put five dots in each
row. Leave 1 inch of space between all the dots.

Here's what you do next. Connect the dots to
make circles. All your circles must have a radius
of 1 inch. How many circles can you draw?

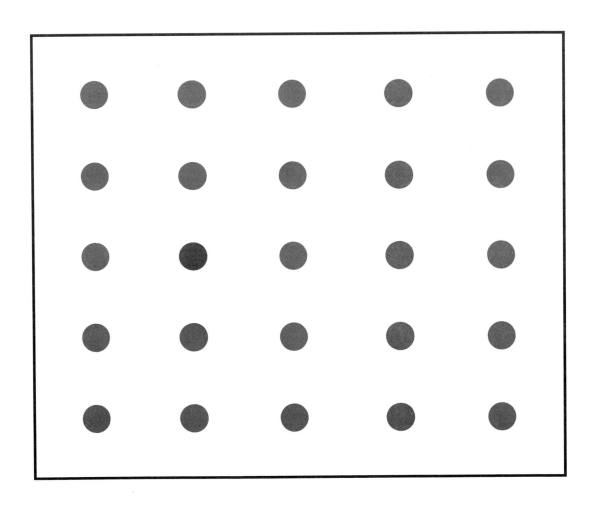

Now see if you can solve this problem about another kind of board—a dart board.

You know that a dart board is circular. Draw one with the numbers 1–16 around the edge of the target. (The board below has been started for you.) The numbers should be evenly spaced. Which number is opposite number 3?

A dart board is a circle. So think about diameters.

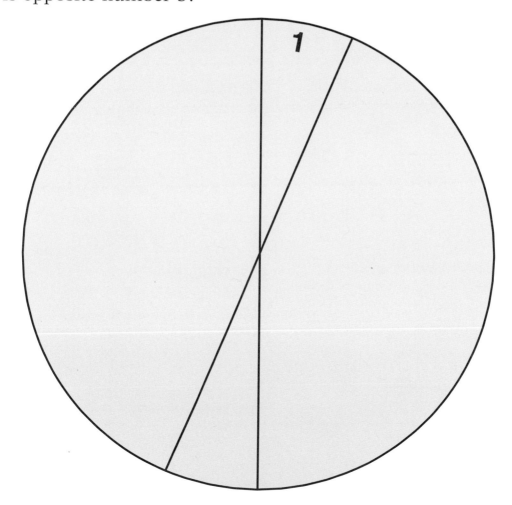

1

Answers

P. 4, Do You Know a Circle When You See One?

In each activity, the circles are the same size.

P. 5, Are Circles Important?

Possible answers: automobile (steering wheel, tires), bike (reflector), clock, dime, eyeglasses, Ferris wheel, goggles, hockey puck, ice-cream container (top), jar (lid), kaleidoscope, camera (lens), medal, nickel, O (the letter), pie, quarter, saucer, thumbtack, yo-yo.

P. 6, Drawing Circles

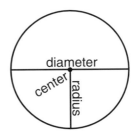

P. 7, Think Fast
1. Eight circles in all.
2. C, D, F, H, I, L are linked.

Pps. 8–9, Compass Creations
No answers.

Pps. 10–11, Wheels and Gears
Gear C turns in a clockwise direction.

P. 12, Can You Get In?
Path 2 leads to the center.

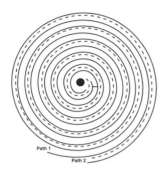

P. 13, A Twisty Circle
1. A twisty loop.
2. Two interlocking loops.

Pps. 14–15, Pedal Power
diameters: DF, EH, FD, HE;
chords: DE, DH, ED, EF, FE, FH, HD, HF; can also accept DF, EH, FD, and HE because diameters are chords;
radii: DS, ES, FS, GS, HS, SD, SE, SF, SG, SH

Pps. 16–17, Tic-Tac-Toe in a Circle
No answers.

Pps. 18–19, What's the Point?
8-point circle: Connecting all points makes an octagon; skipping one point makes a square; skipping two points makes an 8-pointed star.

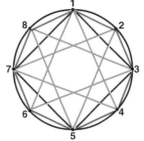

12-point circle: Skipping three points makes a triangle; skipping one point makes a hexagon.

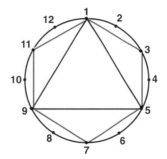

Pps. 20–21, Eyeball Benders
1. B, 2. C, 3. C.
Design B has more blue.

Pps. 22–23, Congruent or Concentric?

There are four pairs of congruent circles. The circles in the other spaces are concentric.

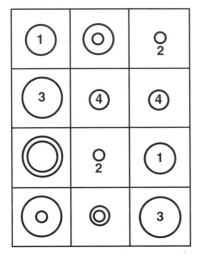

Pps. 24–25, Pizza "Pi"

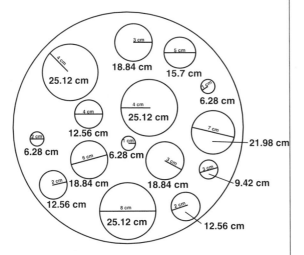

P. 26, Dot and Dart Boards

Dot Board: 9 circles

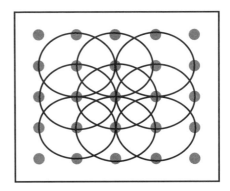

Dart board: The number 11 is opposite number 3.

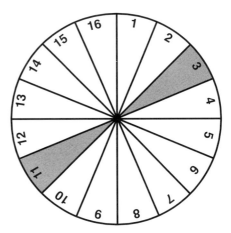

Glossary

chord A line with both end-points on a circle.

Example:

circle A shape in which all points are the same distance from the center point.

circumference The distance around a circle.

clockwise Moving in the direction that the hands of a clock move.

compass A tool for drawing circles. It holds a pencil.

concentric circles Circles that have the same center.

congruent circles Circles that are the same size.

diameter A line that goes through the center of a circle and has both endpoints on the circle.

gear A wheel that has teeth along its outside edge.

hexagon A shape that has six sides.

octagon A shape that has eight sides.

pi The decimal number 3.14. To find the circumference of a circle the diameter is multiplied by pi.

radius A line from the center of a circle to a point on the circle. The plural of radius is radii.

square A shape that has four sides the same length.

triangle A shape that has three sides.

31

Index